# A Day in the Life: Grassland Animals

# Baboon

Louise Spilsbury

**www.raintreepublishers.co.uk**
Visit our website to find out
more information about
Raintree books.

**To order:**
☎ Phone 0845 6044371
🖷 Fax +44 (0) 1865 312263
🖳 Email myorders@raintreepublishers.co.uk

Customers from outside the UK please telephone +44 1865 312262

Raintree is an imprint of Capstone Global Library Limited,
a company incorporated in England and Wales having its
registered office at 7 Pilgrim Street, London, EC4V 6LB
– Registered company number: 6695582

Edited by Dan Nunn, Rebecca Rissman, Catherine Veitch
  and Nancy Dickmann
Designed by Philippa Jenkins
Picture research by Mica Brancic
Originated by Capstone Global Library
Printed and bound in China by South China Printing
Company Ltd

ISBN 978 1 406 21781 0
14 13 12 11 10
10 9 8 7 6 5 4 3 2 1

**British Library Cataloguing in Publication Data**
Spilsbury, Louise.
Baboon. -- (A day in the life. Grassland animals)
599.8'65-dc22
A full catalogue record for this book is available from the
British Library.

**Acknowledgements**
We would like to thank the following for permission to
reproduce photographs: Alamy pp. 6 (© Ulrich Doering), 17
(© Photoshot Holdings Ltd), 18, 23 male (© Paul Springett
01), 22 (© Arco Images GmbH); Corbis p. 5 (© Craig Lovell);
Getty p. 19 (Time & Life Pictures/John Dominis); Photolibrary
p. 21 (Tips Italia); Shutterstock pp. 4 (© urosr), 8 (© Den-
nis Donohue), 9, 23 grassland (© Xtreme safari Inc.), 10, 23
grooming (© Jurie Maree), 11 (© Gert Johannes Jacobus Very),
12 (© Neil Bradfield), 13 (© EcoPrint), 14 (Igor Alyukov), 15,
23 communicate (© dwphotos), 16 (© ShutterVision), 20 (©
Chris Kruger), 23 cliff (© Caitlin Mirra), 23 hyena (© Antonio
Jorge Nunes), 23 insect (kd2).

Cover photograph of a chacma baboon in South Africa
reproduced with permission of Shutterstock (© Chris
Kruger). Back cover photographs of (left) a baboon's snout
reproduced with permission of Alamy (© Ulrich Doering)
and (right) baboons grooming reproduced with permission of
Shutterstock (© Jurie Maree).

We would like to thank Michael Bright for his invaluable help
in the preparation of this book.

The author would like to dedicate this book to her nephew and
niece, Ben and Amelie: "I wrote these books for animal lovers
like you. I hope you enjoy them." Aunty Louise.

Every effort has been made to contact copyright holders
of material reproduced in this book. Any omissions will
be rectified in subsequent printings if notice is given to
the publisher.

All the Internet addresses (URLs) given in this book were valid
at the time of going to press. However, due to the dynamic
nature of the Internet, some addresses may have changed, or
sites may have changed or ceased to exist since publication.
While the author and publisher regret any inconvenience this
may cause readers, no responsibility for any such changes can
be accepted by either the author or the publisher.

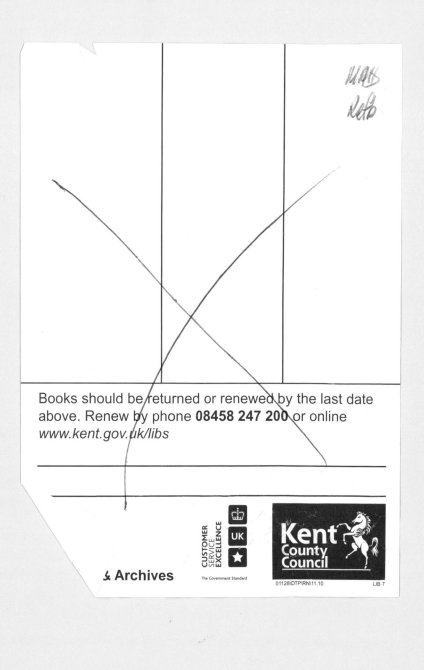

Books should be returned or renewed by the last date above. Renew by phone **08458 247 200** or online *www.kent.gov.uk/libs*

# Contents

Some words are in bold, **like this**. You can find out what they mean by looking in the glossary.

A baboon is a type of monkey.

Baboons are some of the biggest monkeys in the world!

Baboons live in groups of about 50 animals.

Baboons stay together in a group most days and nights.

# What does a baboon look like?

snout

A baboon has big ears, a snout, and small eyes.

It moves around on all fours and can climb trees well.

There are five different types of baboons.

All baboons look similar, but they have different coloured hair.

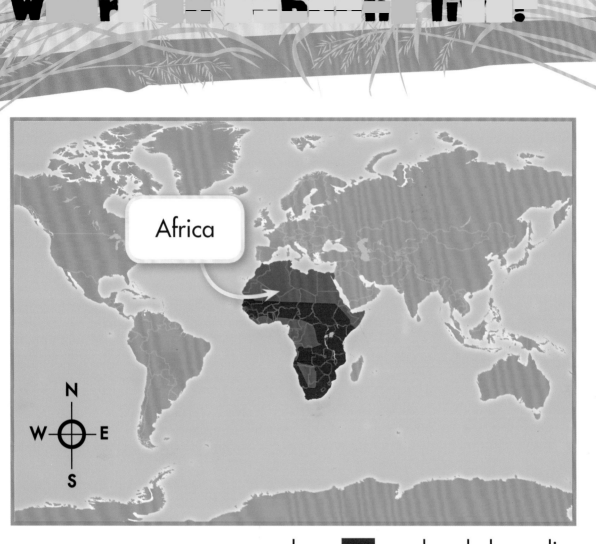

Africa

key: ▪ = where baboons live

Most baboons live in central and southern Africa.

They mostly live in places called **grasslands**.

8

In these grasslands, the land is covered in grasses and a few trees.

Mostly it is hot and dry, but in some months it rains a lot.

Most baboons start the day by **grooming** each other.

They pick dirt and **insects** from each other's hair to keep clean.

After grooming, baboons start to look
for food.

At midday when it gets very hot, they rest
in a shady spot.

# What does it eat and drink?

Baboons mostly eat grasses and other plants.

They sometimes eat small monkeys, spiders, frogs, and insects.

Baboons get some of the water they need from their food.

In the rainy months they drink from pools of water, too.

Baboons **communicate** in different ways across wide **grassland** spaces.

They bark, grunt, roar, and chatter!

Baboons also communicate by smiling or showing their teeth.

By showing its teeth, a baboon warns other baboons it is ready to fight.

# W__t __r _____ babies like?

Baboon babies have black hair that gets lighter as they grow.

At first, the babies stay with their mother, day and night.

Later, young baboons play with each other in the day.

During play times they learn how to run, climb, and fight.

# W i im l nt baboons?

During the day, animals like leopards, lions, and **hyenas** hunt baboons.

Some **male** baboons climb trees to watch for danger.

If a baboon spots danger, it barks.

The other males attack the dangerous animal or chase it away.

# W__t _____ __ at night?

Baboons usually find a different place to sleep every night.

Before they sleep, baboons **groom** each other again.

**cliff** high rock with a very steep side

**communicate** give information or messages to others

**grassland** land where mostly grasses grow

**grooming** when animals clean each other's skin and hair

**hyena** wild animal that mostly lives in grasslands in Africa. It looks like a dog.

**insect** small animal with six legs. Ants, beetles, and bees are insects.

**male** animal that can become a father when it is grown up

# Find out more

## Books

*Apes and Monkeys (Kingfisher Young Knowledge)*,
   Barbara Taylor (Kingfisher, 2007)
*Baboons (Nature Watch)*, Melissa Stewart (Lerner, 2006)
*Baboons: Survivors of the African Continent*, Louise Barratt
   (Dorling Kindersley, 2001)

## Websites

http://animals.nationalgeographic.com/animals/mammals/
   baboon/
http://www.bbc.co.uk/nature/species/Olive_Baboon

## Index